50 THIN
BOOK SERIES
REVIEWS FROM READERS

I recently downloaded a couple of books from this series to read over the weekend thinking I would read just one or two. However, I so loved the books that I read all the six books I had downloaded in one go and ended up downloading a few more today. Written by different authors, the books offer practical advice on how you can perform or achieve certain goals in life, which in this case is how to have a better life.

The information is simple to digest and learn from, and is incredibly useful. There are also resources listed at the end of the book that you can use to get more information.

50 Things To Know To Have A Better Life: Self-Improvement Made Easy! by Dannii Cohen

---

This book is very helpful and provides simple tips on how to improve your everyday life. I found it to be useful in improving my overall attitude.

50 Things to Know For Your Mindfulness & Meditation Journey by Nina Edmondso

---

Quick read with 50 short and easy tips for what to think about before starting to homeschool.

50 Things to Know About Getting Started with Homeschool by Amanda Walton

50 Things to Know

I really enjoyed the voice of the narrator, she speaks in a soothing tone. The book is a really great reminder of things we might have known we could do during stressful times, but forgot over the years.

- HarmonyHawaii

50 Things to Know to Manage Your Stress: Relieve The Pressure and Return The Joy To Your Life

by Diane Whitbeck

There is so much waste in our society today. Everyone should be forced to read this book. I know I am passing it on to my family.

50 Things to Know to Downsize Your Life: How To Downsize, Organize, And Get Back to Basics

by Lisa Rusczyk Ed. D.

Great book to get you motivated and understand why you may be losing motivation. Great for that person who wants to start getting healthy, or just for you when you need motivation while having an established workout routine.

50 Things To Know To Stick With A Workout: Motivational Tips To Start The New You Today

by Sarah Hughes

50 THINGS TO KNOW TO RECHARGE YOUR MIND

Mradula Jain

50 Things to Know

Cover designed by: Ivana Stamenkovic
Cover Image: https://pixabay.com/en/jetty-woman-sitting-relaxing-dock-1834801/

CZYK Publishing Since 2011.

50 Things to Know
Visit our website at www.50thingstoknow..com

Lock Haven, PA
All rights reserved.
ISBN: 9781723980619

50 THINGS TO KNOW TO RECHARGE YOUR MIND

50 Things to Know

BOOK DESCRIPTION

Before starting the book let's have some brain
exercise. Answer below questions with yes or no.

Have you ever felt happy that you kept your thoughts
with only you?

Are you an introvert? If yes then have you ever felt
sad about it?

Did your mind ever stuck in a loop with the same
thoughts?

If you answered yes to any of these questions then
this book is for you...

50 Things To Know To Recharge Your Mind by
Mradula Jain offers an approach to get your mind
refresh and gain positive energy. Most books on
Life tell you to be calm and patient. Although
there's nothing wrong with that, but it takes too
much time to learn that. It is not that easy to
achieve this in just couple of days. Based on
knowledge from the world's leading experts
patience is the key of success but to get this key

one need to practice a lot and then they said that
practice makes a man perfect.

In these pages you'll discover the mantra to recharge
your brain cells. This theory can be treated as
Mind Yoga. This book will help you to understand
about yourself. As per above lines patience leads to
success but for patience one needs to practice and
practice make man perfect but a perfect man can
be or cannot be successful. Hence what I
understood that success belongs to your mind. If
your mind is positive, your life would be positive
which will lead you to success.

By the time you finish this book, you will know that
you have started understanding your mind and you
are now able to recharge it on your own. So grab
YOUR copy today. You'll be glad you did.

TABLE OF CONTENTS

10. If Something is Bothering You, Instead of Panicking Try To Analyze the Root Cause

11. If You Feel Nervous Just Keep Your Mind Empty/Thoughtless and Then You Will Feel Confident

12. If You Feel Sad Just Hug Someone and If You Don't Have Anyone Then Give a Tight Hug to Your Pillow/Teddy Bear

13. If You Feel Nostalgic and Feel Like Crying, Then Cry, You Will Feel Light

14. If You Are Feeling Lazy Do Yoga/Exercise Whenever You Get Time

15. If You Feel Bored With Your Studies, Read About Your Favorite Topic or Do Your Most Favorite Thing

16. If You Got Flunked in Your Exam Then Remember This is Not End of Your Life

17. If You Are Bored With Your Work Then Find A Hobby

18. If There Are Problems in Your Work Life Then Take Break For A Day Or A Week And Go For Vacation

19. To Solve Issues Between You And Your Family/Friends All You Need To Do is Start Listening Others Too

20. If You Are Mentally or Physically Challenged Then Think About Some Unusual Things Which You Can Only Do
21. If You Are Worried About Your Kids Upbringing Then Spend Time With Them
22. If You Have Lost Your Parents Then Help Others to Understand Their Value
23. To Deal With Short Temper Try to be Quite
24. If You Are in Pain Then Shout Out Loud
25. Try to Mould Situation According to You And If You Know That You Are Not That Capable Enough Then Ignore
26. Stop Expecting, Start Appreciating
27. Be Confident Enough to Introduce Who You Are
28. No Matter How Hard The Situation is, There is Always A Key For Every Lock
29. Give 10 Minutes Daily to You to Think About Yourself
30. In The Mid Of Every Year Analyze Yourself And Compare Your Growth With Last Year. If Count is Zero This Year Then Start Working towards this.
31. If There is a Huge Business Loss Then Think About Yourself. You Only Made This Business, Business Did Not Make You and Hence You Can Make it Again

32. If You Are Getting Continuous Rejections in Interview Then That Job is Not For You.

33. Before Breaking Any Relationship Think Twice That Why You Were Still There

34. If You Have Recently Broke Up And It is Now Hurting You Then Before Start Crying Think Why Did You Break Up

35. If You Have Lost Something Then Believe Me it Was Not Yours

36. If Nobody Respects You Then First You Start Respecting Yourself. Always Have Self Respect

37. If You Desire Something, Write it Dawn on Daily Basis, Trust Me It Would Be Yours Very Soon

38. Stop Comparing, Start Respecting

39. When You Feel Happy, Go To Temple/Church/Muszid And When You Are Sad Go To Orphanages/Old Age Homes

40. Speak Only When it is Necessary. The More You Listen, The More You Save Your Energy

41. Everyday Make an Aim And Try to Fulfill it Without Any Fail

42. Talk To Your Grand Parents Once in a While And Simply Enjoy Their Experiences About Life

43. Try To Help A Needy One on Daily Basis or Whenever possible

DEDICATION

My monotonous routine made me realize that I need to do something to get my mind recharged and that's how I got inspired with my own daily life. When I started conveying my thoughts to others, they found it helpful and that's how I got dedicated to write them all in a book.

50 Things to Know

ABOUT THE AUTHOR

Time flies, true. I was 14 when my dad got heart fail and then our family started struggling financially. My grandmother got sick and my Mom was the only backbone left in the family as me and my siblings were too young to handle responsibilities. That time was the worst time of my life but I remembered that my dad always used to say "Which happens to be good" and then I started finding a good in that situation. Earlier I and my mom were having differences but after dad's death we came closer. Which was very first positive though I could have gathered that time and then I thought if I can find a good even in this worse, nothing can make me feel down. Since that time I always try to opt a good in a bad and gradually this all theory helped me to keep my mind recharged.

Currently I work with an IT organization as a Software Developer.

I find myself on social media below:

https://www.facebook.com/mradulajain247

https://twitter.com/R0cking_MJ

https://mradulaforyou.blogspot.com/

https://www.linkedin.com/in/mradulajain/

50 Things to Know

INTRODUCTION

Addiction is the most dangerous thing in this world. We all are addicted to something or someone. Knowingly or unknowingly our whole life surrounds with our addiction.

Once we are used to of anything, it is very tough to get rid of. Even if you don't want still your mind process those thoughts again and again. This is where you need to recharge your mind so that you can overcome with those thoughts which are harmful for you and your body.

This book introduces about mind and its behavior. Whatever we think that is exactly how we start feel. Hence for a positive life it is very important to keep your mind under your control and for that we need to recharge our mind time to time. This book will help you to achieve it by explaining different behaviors of mind and how you can deal with them.

50 Things to Know

1. WHENEVER YOU FEEL MOOD SWINGS TRY TO UNDERSTAND YOUR THOUGHTS

Sometimes we feel happy for no reason and so vice verse other times. This all happens because of our mood swings. Some may have a little but some may have this as major problem. Sometimes we can even loose our temper and regret later on.

Start understanding your thoughts whenever you get such mood swings. The root cause of mood swings is nothing but our own consistent thoughts and when we over think we get these mood swings. If we try to understand what exactly we want, we can work on that direction and even if that is not possible to get still we can have satisfaction that we tried but even after trying one is not able to get it then start doing some other things parallel. This will definitely help you control mood swings and recharge your mind.

2. WHEN YOU ARE ANGRY DRINK CHILLED WATER

Well its very common phenomenon that we all lose temper. Some may lose in very short and some may belong to a calm club where it takes a very crucial situation to get mad on but all and all nobody is there in this world who does not get angry.

To control anger there is no way except meditation and while angry we may say so many bad words to others and it is very tough to control your words in that situation so the best way to deal with this, is drink chilled water whenever you are angry. This will definitely reduce your temper by 50-70% and this will help you to have a better image in public as well as for inner you.

3. IF YOU FEEL LOW JUST SLEEP

It is not necessary to have a good day all time. Sometimes it gets bad and sometimes even worst. If our day is like that then we feel low.

Whenever you feel low just sleep because while feeling low we feel all kind of pain we have already gone through in past and this is really not good to remember those bad days while you are having already one. So the best therapy during such situations is to sleep. After a sound sleep you will feel refresh and energetic and that feeling of lowness will definitely would be controlled as your brain got refreshed.

4. WHEN YOU FEEL ALONE TALK TO YOURSELF

There are many situations occur in our daily lives where we can easily feel lonely. This is because we are not closer to family or friends or partner. We all need someone in our lives may be human or a pet to talk about our day and if we don't get one, we start feeling alone.

If there is no one to talk then write your own thoughts. This will help you to understand what you want, how your day went and how do you feel. If you are not a writing person or if you don't have much time to write then start talking to yourself. Nobody knows you better then you then why don't you talk to yourself. Don't worry it doesn't sound stupid. May be people can laugh on you but nothing wrong in that.

We always need someone to talk and if you don't have one, be the one, that too for yourself.

5. WHEN YOU FEEL HAPPY TRY NOT TO EXPRESS SO MUCH

Always try to keep your success with you only. Of course success is the thing to show off but make sure that there are many people out there getting jealous and that jealousy produces negative vibes which may affect your positive successful environment.

Always priorities your surrounding according to your thoughts. After all you can not share everything with everyone.

6. WHEN YOU FEEL DEPRESSED TALK TO AS MANY PEOPLE AS YOU CAN

When you feel depressed or sad talk to as many people as you can but make sure you always don't talk about you try to listen them as well this will help you to heal while you will be listening others you will start thinking that not only you but so many other people are also suffering from their problems.

While talking, try not to always talk about your problems instead talk about your blessings more. This will give you strength to fight with your odds.

7. WHEN YOU ARE HUNGRY AND THERE IS NOTHING TO EAT OF YOUR CHOICE DRINK WATER

There may be days in office on weekends or during late night when you are out and you are hungry and there is nothing to eat, drink water. While drinking make sure you take 2-3 sips at a time and then take a break for at least 5-10 minutes for next couple of sips. This will help you to fight with your hunger.

Although it is not a good habit so always make sure if you are going out keep some handy food with you or at least take some candies they contain sugar which helps to fight with hunger.

8. WHEN YOU WANT ARE TIRED AND STILL BOUNDED TO WORK JUST CLOSE YOUR EYES AND RUB THEM, TAKE 3 DEEP BREATHS AND RESUME YOUR WORK

In IT culture it is very common to stretch beyond your limits many times. In such situations try to take a nap for 20 minutes. This will help your brain to recharge and if you don't have even 20 minutes for yourself then take your chair down backside, close your eyes for a while and take 3 deep breaths. This will reduce your stress and then rub your eyes from both of your hands and then open slowly. This will definitely help you to resume your work with some fresh thoughts and positive energy.

9. WHEN IT IS TOUGH TO CONCENTRATE, THINK THE NEXT MOST THING YOU WANT TO DO

Sometimes it is really tough to concentrate on your current work. In such cases think about the very next most thing you want to do, may be you have a date in some time or you want to go home and want to take a hot bubble bath or it could be anything like that pie in you fridge which you have waited for entire day. Just think about the joy you will be getting while doing that but before reaching there you need to complete this current task and that's how it will help you to concentrate.

10. IF SOMETHING IS BOTHERING YOU, INSTEAD OF PANICKING TRY TO ANALYZE THE ROOT CAUSE

It is very common if something bothers you. There could be so many reasons behind your panic but instead of getting worried try to figure out the reason behind that panic. Always try to analyze the situation and the problem with that situation, that problem would be the root cause of your panic. Try to fix that and that is how your brain would be recharged and ready to fight with other issues.

11. IF YOU FEEL NERVOUS JUST KEEP YOUR MIND EMPTY/THOUGHTLESS AND THEN YOU WILL FEEL CONFIDENT

It doesn't matter whether it is a big presentation or a college viva, a life changing moment or a simple thought to execute, if you are feeling nervous then this is because you have so many positive and negative thoughts there in your brain. Your brain is feeling so much under pressure. Always remember one thing that pressure works only for inside stuff to be cooked and it always should be balanced. More pressure can cause overheated food whereas less pressure makes it non cooked.

So always try to make a good balance in your brain and if you fail in that just try to keep your mind empty. No thoughts at all, just go and give your best without any kind of fear. I can not assure that this will take you on top but I bet that this will boost your confidence and this confidence can help you to top.

12. IF YOU FEEL SAD JUST HUG SOMEONE AND IF YOU DON'T HAVE ANYONE THEN GIVE A TIGHT HUG TO YOUR PILLOW/TEDDY BEAR

Hug therapy is one of the best way to deal with stress and depression. Trust me it helps to recover from all kind of anxiety. I know it is practically not possible that you can have someone near you every time when you need hug, so keep it simple and try to hug your teddy bear or pillow or any other object which is closer to you and this will certainly help you to fight with all those bad feelings and will refresh your mind.

13. IF YOU FEEL NOSTALGIC AND FEEL LIKE CRYING, THEN CRY, YOU WILL FEEL LIGHT

It happens many times when we feel homesick or nostalgic. In such cases it is really good to let your feelings flow in form of tears. There is nothing bad in that. We all cry at times and it is not a sign of weakness. This is a way to get your mind recharge for other usual things. If something makes you cry then cry and let that feeling out from your heart.

14. IF YOU ARE FEELING LAZY DO YOGA/EXERCISE WHENEVER YOU GET TIME

Well indeed I am a lazy bone person and I hate it when it comes to walk or running or exercise. If you are also one then make sure this habit is not gonna work in long way. You have to be active towards your body and life style if you want a healthy future. I understand that it is really tough to manage a routine but try to do it whenever you get time. This will help you to be fresh and active.

Maintain a healthy lifestyle is really nice for your health if you are already managing one then you are in safe zone if not then start doing yoga/exercise/dancing whatever you like it will help you to refresh your body and bring that energy back.

15. IF YOU FEEL BORED WITH YOUR STUDIES, READ ABOUT YOUR FAVORITE TOPIC OR DO YOUR MOST FAVORITE THING

As a student we all feel like the entire boredom is hidden under our books. So whenever you are just got bored with same old study material, try to read your kind of books which contains your taste. If you are not a reading person then do your most favorite thing sometime and then resume your main studies. This will help you to focus on your study well.

16. IF YOU GOT FLUNKED IN YOUR EXAM THEN REMEMBER THIS IS NOT END OF YOUR LIFE

This happens in many cases where if we get flunked in our exam then it hurts a lot. It doesn't matter if that is an entrance exam or university exam or some regular school exam. In such kind of situations do make sure that this is not end of your life. Life is not that short, you still have so many chances to prove yourself. All you need to do is to prepare well for next. Never lose your hopes because hope is one of the most important parameters for success.

17. IF YOU ARE BORED WITH YOUR WORK THEN FIND A HOBBY

If you got bored with your same usual routine work/life, then my friend it is time to find a hobby. This can be anything in which you take interest. Anything which makes you happy. This hobby will recharge your mind and you will be back to your work with a fresh mind.

18. IF THERE ARE PROBLEMS IN YOUR WORK LIFE THEN TAKE BREAK FOR A DAY OR A WEEK AND GO FOR VACATION

A break is always a good way to recharge your mind. This break could be from anything, whether it is from study or from work or from your daily usual life. Whenever you feel like there are problems and you neither want to face them nor are they getting solved in such cases best way to get relief is to go for an outing or a trip.

Plan accordingly to your budget, mood and time. Even I used to have so much pressure during my office days and then I used to take a day off and trust me that used to help me to handle that all pressure. Same thing applies to your college life whenever exams are coming just take a day off without study and energize you to study for next entire week. I know it is tough to implement but I used to do this and it helped me during my studies.

19. TO SOLVE ISSUES BETWEEN YOU AND YOUR FAMILY/FRIENDS ALL YOU NEED TO DO IS START LISTENING OTHERS TOO

Whenever there is a fight it is because nobody wants listen. All of us just simply blame each others. We communicate to blame not to understand. First start listening and then you start to see and feel the difference that how this affects your mind in a positive way. All you need to do is to before saying anything from your side just listen what others want to say to you. This helps to save relationships as well as your energy.

20. IF YOU ARE MENTALLY OR PHYSICALLY CHALLENGED THEN THINK ABOUT SOME UNUSUAL THINGS WHICH YOU CAN ONLY DO

There is nothing in this world which a human can not do it is all about will power. If you want to do that, you will definitely do that. When it comes to physically challenged people they all have some special characteristics which make them unique. Like a blind person has a stronger sense of touch than a normal person. A person with physical disability usually blessed with a great brain. They can think and learn way faster than normal human being. It is all about your will power. Never underestimate yourself.

21. IF YOU ARE WORRIED ABOUT YOUR KIDS UPBRINGING THEN SPEND TIME WITH THEM

There may be so precious things in this world but for parents their kids are priceless. Nothing can be compared with their kids. Parents do every possible and impossible thing to make their kids happy. Now-a-days kids are getting away from family values. They don't feel comfortable when family is around. This is because they didn't get this all since beginning.

Make sure whatever they do or reacts in their teenage or adult, it is just a reflection of their upbringing. Make sure you spend as much time as you can with your kids or else you are going to lose them in future. Listen them, talk to them and when it needed guide them. Kids are like clay the way you will mould, they will be like that only. So make sure about your every step towards them.

22. IF YOU HAVE LOST YOUR PARENTS THEN HELP OTHERS TO UNDERSTAND THEIR VALUE

Many of us are blessed with parents whereas many others are not. I feel sad for me when I see any father daughter duo. I start missing my dad and if you can feel the same then start making other realize that what they have and why they should value it. The one who respects parents is the one with great moral values.

If somebody does so much for you but not respecting his/her parents, I am telling you that never trust such person because if someone is not respecting his/her parents then he/she can not respect anyone in this world. If they are respecting you then trust me it is all temporary. It will pass with time.

If you know such kind of person who have parents and they don't respect them then talk to them and explain that how they are going to suffer without them. This will make you satisfied.

23. TO DEAL WITH SHORT TEMPER TRY TO BE QUITE

Short temper is a very major problem in today's life. Everybody wants to say but nobody wants to listen and this is why temper takes place. Short temper is very dangerous; one can even kill someone during that. Because when we are angry it is really tough to differentiate between right and wrong. In such cases it is a very good practice to be quite. It will not only save your energy but also it will help you to grow personally. Once you start practicing you will feel the change.

24. IF YOU ARE IN PAIN THEN SHOUT OUT LOUD

Pain can be in many types. It could be physically, mentally and emotionally. When something is hurting your body then you feel it physically, while disturbed then mentally and when vulnerable from inside then you feel it emotionally. Now irrespective of any kind of pain, whenever you feel it just shout out loud. This will help you to flush out your frustration towards your pain and then you will feel like crying and this will help you to overcome things. Some people even don't cry, they just shout and feel light. Try it, you will be amazed.

25. TRY TO MOULD SITUATION ACCORDING TO YOU AND IF YOU KNOW THAT YOU ARE NOT THAT CAPABLE ENOUGH THEN IGNORE

In any kind of difficult situation try to mould things according to you. Try your best to get things under control and if this all is not happening and you know that this could not be controlled anymore then start ignoring things. Just go with the flow as you can not help it anymore. You have done your best and now nothing can be done from your side. There is a limit in this world for everything and after that limit you can not change anything.

26. STOP EXPECTING, START APPRECIATING

Start appreciating as much as you can. People who expect a lot are looser because they don't do anything on their own instead expect it to be done from someone else. This does not go long way. Firstly stop expecting too much this will not take you anywhere except shame. Start appreciate others, this will cost you nothing but will help you to create a positive environment around you which will give you a new thought process towards life.

27. BE CONFIDENT ENOUGH TO INTRODUCE WHO YOU ARE

Never be ashamed about your identity. Your identity introduces you and it is very important in any area that people know the real you. There is nothing wrong if you work in a small shop or as a waiter. Also it doesn't matter if you are disabled or you have some sexual disorder. These are not the parameter to judge you. Always judge a person on the basis of their nature and attitude towards life and other people

and if someone judges you on your job or home or
lifestyle then make sure then certainly he/she is not
the one you should spend your precious time with.

28. NO MATTER HOW HARD THE SITUATION IS, THERE IS ALWAYS A KEY FOR EVERY LOCK

Start learning from each and every incident, no
matter it is tiny or huge. There is always a learning in
everything all you need is to understand and analyze
it well. This will help you whenever you stuck in any
situation/problem. Problems usually occur due to lack
of resources, miscommunications or bad/no planning.
Whenever any problem occurs, try to find a solution
instead of blaming.

Try to find the reason why it happened as
sometimes it may help you to resolve the issue. In
some cases the backtracking is not required as it does
not matter how much you go deeper it will never give
you a solution, in such cases one should always try to
find the solution instead of backtrack the problem.

29. GIVE 10 MINUTES DAILY TO YOU TO THINK ABOUT YOURSELF

Always try to find some time for yourself. It is very important that you should know about you, your needs and how do you feel. You should always be your priority. No matter how hard it is but always tries to save some time for you. Even 10 minutes on daily basis would be good if you can do that. All you need is just observe your day and think over it that how did it go, is this the way you wanted it to be, are you happy/satisfied your day.

If answers are yes then it is you way to go. You are doing what you want in your life but if answers are no then start thinking over it that how come you can be the one who can make you happy and can make your life the way you want it to be. At the end of the day it should be you who needs to be happy from you. If you are not able to make yourself happy then start working in that direction. It will definitely help you to grow.

30. IN THE MID OF EVERY YEAR ANALYZE YOURSELF AND COMPARE YOUR GROWTH WITH LAST YEAR. IF COUNT IS ZERO THIS YEAR THEN START WORKING TOWARDS THIS.

You should hold some growth every year. If your growth is nothing as compared to last year then you are at zero this year. This is a very major factor we all should understand that we all should always try to keep motivated ourselves that we can do better than this. Satisfaction in life is very important but satisfaction of your growth should never be there. One should always be active about their personal growth.

In the start of the year always try to set some goals for you and try to analyze at the mid of the year that how long have you been there. If you are half way done then you are doing well. If not even half way then you need to work harder to reach to your goals. If you are about to done then congrats you can enjoy your new year with a better personality.

31. IF THERE IS A HUGE BUSINESS LOSS THEN THINK ABOUT YOURSELF. YOU ONLY MADE THIS BUSINESS, BUSINESS DID NOT MAKE YOU AND HENCE YOU CAN MAKE IT AGAIN

Sometimes it happens that in just one night an entire empire has broke and the businessman has lost his mind and there is nothing wrong in that, it is like last night you slept as a billionaire and this morning you have nothing in your hand.

I know it is really tough to deal such kind of situation though I never faced one still I can imagine how it could be. Well all I can say is that business is from you, you are not from business. You only made it once so you can make it again. I know it is easy to say such words but it is tremendously tough to achieve but it was tough earlier as well and you achieved it there and hence you can do it again all you need is that same will power and strength to fulfill your dream.

32. IF YOU ARE GETTING CONTINUOUS REJECTIONS IN INTERVIEW THEN THAT JOB IS NOT FOR YOU.

Well I know it is very rude to say that this thing is not for you but my friend it is very true that some people are not made for some things, they are made for some better things than they even think of. Like if you are constantly failing in any exam then that is certainly not for you. You should try something in which you are really interested and if that exam is of your interest then my friend you need to better understand your interest.

If you are not able to crack any job interview or any audition or failure in your start up/business then you should keep trying until you are done with your tries. Once you are done then make sure that you are done and now you will start something better and new but this one again as you have already tried your best and it is the time to move on completely.

33. BEFORE BREAKING ANY RELATIONSHIP THINK TWICE THAT WHY YOU WERE STILL THERE

Now-a-days it is very common to have a relationship. It is very important that our thoughts should be matched. Even if they not then at least there should be the one who can respect our thoughts and not in every relationship we find someone like that but if you have found someone like that and now you want to break that relationship then think twice that is it really important to break it up.

Let's take my own example. I was in the relationship with this guy and then due to some ego issues I broke up with him, then we patched up and then again broke up and patched up. This happen thrice and then we realized that there is something between us which won't let us apart. Also we were happy together but due to some family situations we broke up thrice and in the end we decided that no matter what happened we won't leave each other.

We were in long distance relationship, first national and then international. So there were time differences, work pressure and so many other things. It was getting worst day by day but we both had faith and then somehow situation changed, our families came in support in our decision and eventually we got married.

So trust me it is very tough to find one with same mental disorder and it is even tougher to find someone who is not as mental as you, still try to understand your mentality. If you have one, don't let them go.

34. IF YOU HAVE RECENTLY BROKE UP AND IT IS NOW HURTING YOU THEN BEFORE START CRYING THINK WHY DID YOU BREAK UP

Sometimes in relationship it is more important to take a stand for yourself and if you are in such kind of situation and you broke up because of that, then my friend you did it right. Self respect is the most important thing for you and one is not able to respect you then he/she is not a keeper. Don't waste your time they don't deserve you.

If you are thinking to do a break up or you have just broke up then you should feel sad about it and if you are feeling so then think over the issues again due to those you broke up. This will make you realize that your decision was right. You have to stand for you and you took right decision on right time. Never blame yourself for a breakup if it was coming on self respect. Nobody can disrespect you, not even you. Always remember that you are worth it.

35. IF YOU HAVE LOST SOMETHING THEN BELIEVE ME IT WAS NOT YOURS

Well I would say lose is lose, it doesn't matter it is money lose or something theft or lost. Always keep one thing in your mind that whatever has been lost, was never yours. If something is yours it will come to you no matter how, when or why. There is no power in this world who can take your slice from you. All you need is to understand what is yours and what you desire.

36. IF NOBODY RESPECTS YOU THEN FIRST YOU START RESPECTING YOURSELF. ALWAYS HAVE SELF RESPECT

As I told in earlier steps that self respect is the thing you should never compromise. If you are at the place where no one respects you then I may say that you only don't show respect to yourself there. First start respecting yourself then only you should expect respect from others. One, who could not respect himself, would not be able to get it from others. You always should respect to your identity, your personality and to yourself.

37. IF YOU DESIRE SOMETHING, WRITE IT DAWN ON DAILY BASIS, TRUST ME IT WOULD BE YOURS VERY SOON

The very famous book secret says that whatever you want from universe, just write it down on daily basis and this will create positive energy also the universe will know about your desires and that is how all the universe will help you to achieve it.

My theory behind this sentence is, if you write something on daily basis and you actually need it, those words reminds you to start working in the direction to get this done. You will not know how come you started on your own and after some day it just happened to you. This all happened because you gathered all your positive energy in that direction and it helped a lot.

38. STOP COMPARING, START RESPECTING

Comparison is never good. One should never compare with other. We are not aware about their struggles all we can see is their success. Behind every success there is a story which tell a lot about the situation that person has been through. It is very tough to feel that just by listening. Hence never ever compare yourself with others. Appreciate whatever you have, some may have more than you but some may have less than yours.

Start respecting everyone without any expectation. It is not a good practice that you respect a person just purposely and when it is done you do not respect them anymore. Never have such practice where you are constantly suffering from moral values. We all are blessed with a human being and we should respect humanity.

39. WHEN YOU FEEL HAPPY, GO TO TEMPLE/CHURCH/MUSZID AND WHEN YOU ARE SAD GO TO ORPHANAGES/OLD AGE HOMES

Whenever you feel happy, you should always thank to god that he blessed you with your desire. Although we should always thank god for everything we are blessed with but usually we forget to do so but it is really a good practice to be humble for all your blessings.

The day when you feel extremely happy you should go to temple/church/muszid to thank god for the day where you felt like this. Whatever you feel good or bad is all because of your karma. So you should always be ready for both and never blame god for your odds. The more you thank the more you get.

Whenever you are sad you should go to orphanages/old age homes to see that there are people lower than you, still they are living their lives. They are not blessed with the joy as you are but still they are happy with whatever they have. They know about the karma that when they were having everything they didn't value it and now karma is showing them the other side of life.

40. SPEAK ONLY WHEN IT IS NECESSARY. THE MORE YOU LISTEN, THE MORE YOU SAVE YOUR ENERGY

Listening is the most powerful strength one can have. If you are a good listener, you will gradually develop the power to analyze things/situations quickly. As you speak less and listen more, you gain more and more knowledge about a person or situation and this helps you to understand details about it. The other advantage of listening is that the less you speak the more you save your energy. Also if you speak less and listen more the chances of fight in any communication drastically reduce. So from now choose your energy wisely.

41. EVERYDAY MAKE AN AIM AND TRY TO FULFILL IT WITHOUT ANY FAIL

Apart from the goal setting for entire year, you should try to make an aim every day. In Jainism we call it "Niyam/Saugandh" this is the way to be devoted for something. For an instance suppose for me aim for the day is that I won't lie, so for today no matter what I will try to fulfill my aim without any fail. I will try my best to complete my aim.

You should set your daily aim as per your wish and availability of resources around you. Like if you aim that you won't eat chicken today then you should be prepared for other options like salad or soups on which you can rely for the day and can complete your aim.

42. TALK TO YOUR GRAND PARENTS ONCE IN A WHILE AND SIMPLY ENJOY THEIR EXPERIENCES ABOUT LIFE

Grandparents are treasure that not everybody has. If you have, then enjoy till it lasts. There is always fun in their stories of their lives. They will tell you about their struggles and the way they brought up. They will tell their experience of life which will blow your mind that your adventure is nothing in front of them. They are real hero, they are real gems.

Have some time from your busy schedule and visit them, spend some quality time with them and learn about life. If you are not able to meet then try to connect them via phone or video call. They will be happy to listening you or to see you. Their smile will give you immense satisfaction. This will help you to grow as a humble person with high moral values.

43. TRY TO HELP A NEEDY ONE ON DAILY BASIS OR WHENEVER POSSIBLE

"A friend in need is a friend indeed" is a famous say and it is really justified in all of our cases I can say. We all have so many friends but that one friend who helps us in every difficult situation is the one for us. We usually help our family and friends selflessly but why only them why not the others?

Start to help the needy ones, no matter whether he/she is a human being or an animal. We are humans and humanity is our religion. Follow your religion and try to help a needy one on daily basis. If somebody needs your help in work do it, if someone is hungry, feed them no matter whether they are human or animal. Everybody wants to eat. Hence start with food, try to give food to needy ones.

44. NO MATTER WHAT ALWAYS TRY TO BE KIND TO YOURSELF

It is good to be kind to others but it is most important to be kind to you first. If you are kind to you, you can be kind with everyone. Pushing yourself beyond your limits to get something done is good but punishing yourself that you had not made it, is really bad.

You should not harm yourself in any situation. No matter what always be kind to yourself and try to be happy. I know that to reach somewhere you need to get out of your comfort zone but make sure this all should not affect your body because how would you be able to work if you body is not well. So always make sure that in any situation be kind to you. Pamper you a lot, after all you are the one who is working this hard, so treat yourself is not a bad idea.

45. ALWAYS KEEP A BEST FRIEND WITH YOU

So we all need someone to talk about our lives. Someone trustworthy, caring and who loves us. Of course our parents do that for us but sometimes there are some limitations occur that we can not discuss everything with our parents or siblings. In such times best friends come in picture. Friends are part of our lives. Everybody have friends with whom they feel comfortable and relaxed.

Always keep a best friend with you, with whom you can be you. There should be no filters while talking, you can tell everything to them. The way you feel, think everything can be shared without fear of being judged. Friends don't judge you, they create a positive environment where you can do whatever you like and you can be mad or can say anything.

Your best friend can be anyone, your parents/siblings (if you are very open to them), your pet, your school/college/office mates anyone can be your best friend. You know if you are shy and it for you it is tough to be too much expressive then a book can also be your best friend. Also you can write your thoughts in a dairy and that dairy can be your best friend. Many options are there; just embrace one of your choices.

46. IF YOU HAVE A HABIT OF OVER THINKING THEN START THINKING ABOUT OVER THINKING

Ohh yeah, it's a bit tough to understand here what I want to say. Well let me give you one example, suppose you are on a boat in a full moon night, floating slowly, breezing is relaxing you and now you want to sleep but suddenly one thought about that colleague comes in your mind and you start thinking over it.

Now you are trapped with that thought and now are imagining all negative things he/she did to you. Now you are angry and you are going to ruin your beautiful night just because of that one thought. That single click of fight gave you so many thoughts and then you started floating in thoughts instead of water.

This is called over thinking where you kill your time in chain of never ending thoughts. So whenever you stuck in such kind of situation try to think about this over thinking that why are you thinking about it? Does it really make sense now to rethink over it or it

is just killing my precious time. Then you will be free
from over thinking and mind will be recharged.

47. START TAKING OWNERSHIP OF YOUR OWN HAPPINESS

It is the best thing in this world to love you. If you
know how to love and pamper yourself then you need
no one to be happy in this world. You should be the
owner of your own happiness. You are responsible
for your deeds. Whether they are good or bad, the
fruit is always yours.

Stop thinking that someone is the reason of your
happiness and if you feel so then make sure to change
this habit ASAP. If that person will leave you, you
would be vulnerable so please be kind to yourself and
think over it that you should not give the right to
someone else to be the reason of your joy. It is your
life; make it happy for you on your own.

Treat yourself the way to love to. If you are a
girl/lady you love chocolates, but them; you want to
go to parlor, go there get your things done, do
whatever you want but just be happy. For guys I
know there are some few things if they get, they feel
happy, then try for them and make yourself happy but

make sure you don't hurt other's sentiments while making yourself happy.

48. DREAM HIGH, AIM HIGH

Apart from those daily aims which I asked you to take, you also should aim for yourself according to your needs and your dreams. Your dreams should always be big, "the huge you think, the better you get" so it doesn't matter if you are rich or poor you should always dream big so that you can aim high.

You can reach on top with a big dream and a big aim only. If you are aware about your needs and you know how to fulfill them then you should dream for something else. Something which you can not achieve, always dream about that, this will give you inspiration to do something extraordinary. If you are aiming high and you are able to grow in the right direction you should always be conscious about your thoughts, your words and your deeds.

49. SURROUND YOURSELF WITH POSITIVE PEOPLE AND IF YOU DO NOT FIND ONE THEN BE ONE

The world is full of helping people, if you can't find one, then be one. A famous and beautiful thought which may help us to grow in right direction. Always try to be positive and always try to surround yourself with positive people. Every person has some good quality, all you need to explore them for their good.

When you surround yourself with positive thoughts, you also feel positive and energetic. This energy helps you to grow in right direction. If you do not find any positive person or energy around you then be one.

50. IF YOU ARE DONE WITH YOUR LIFE, DEDICATE IT TO SOMEONE WHO NEEDS IT

And now last but not the least. So many things I have told you to do but now it is the most important part because if this ends there would be nothing. Life, it is very beautiful gift we all got from our parents and some waste it as if it is a Burdon on them. Parents give their best to protect you from the world. They do every possible or impossible thing to make you happy. They sacrifice their lives for you so that they can give you everything you want. If you being to a rich family then think about the time your parents gave you.

We all live ones, so why wasting it in suicide and any other crime. Why are you taking this life as a Burdon on you, why you want to kill it? Why are you seeing it negatively? Is it this bad? If yes then think about those who are orphan and have nothing with them. If you are orphan then think about the people with disability, if you are disable then think about that one thing which makes your life different from others. We all have something special in us; all we need is to recognize it.

Life is precious do not commit suicide or any other crime to ruin it. You have an opportunity to make this amazing world more beautiful, so please don't waste that. Don't waste your time and energy in negative thoughts, make yourself positive and make your surrounding positive. You have that power to do. You are the hero of your life. Nothing is impossible for you. You can make this world a better place. You can do whatever you want. Just think about it and start working towards the best possible contribution you can give to this planet.

Life is precious not only ours but everybody else's as well. So please don't let anybody else too ruin their lives. Try to bring them on right path and if you are not able to do that then at least be a good example to follow so that they can refer you and can try to be the better version of themselves.

To write articles about life and experiences is easy but when it comes to facing problems it is way tougher than it appears. Giving advice is always easier than implementing. Always try to implement your advice first, so that would be no longer an advice then that would be an example and people follow examples not the advice.

After reading this book if still you are not convinced about your valuable life and its importance then instead of committing a sin try to give yourself to someone else. Dedicate your whole life to someone whom you want to take care of. This someone could be anything or anyone. This will give your life a whole new direction, sense of satisfaction, a new hope to life and an amazing joy to your soul and peace of your mind.

Well these all were my thoughts towards life where I was trying to make this world beautiful by my words as this is the best way to convey message. As I told you I am blogger so you can read my blogs where you can find so many positive creations about life and its beauty.

50 Things to Know

Apart from this book you can find some other sources as well where you can get some ideas to recharge your mind. Below are the references:

Title: Lifehack
https://www.lifehack.org/articles/productivity/10-surprisingly-simple-things-you-can-recharge-your-mind.html

Title: Inc
https://www.inc.com/jayson-demers/7-ways-to-recharge-your-mind-midday.html

Title: HUFFPOST
https://www.huffingtonpost.com/matthew-edlund-md/no-time-for-downtime-gett_b_698530.html

Title: Thrive Global
https://medium.com/thrive-global/the-cure-for-stress-3-steps-to-recharge-your-brain-and-your-life-part-2-3a9803678ee8

50 Things to Know

READ OTHER
50 THINGS TO KNOW
BOOKS

50 Things to Know

50 Things to Know

Website: 50thingstoknow.com

Facebook: facebook.com/50thingstoknow

Pinterest: pinterest.com/lbrennec

YouTube: youtube.com/user/50ThingsToKnow

Twitter: twitter.com/50ttk

Mailing List: Join the 50 Things to Know
   Mailing List to Learn About New Releases

50 Things to Know

50 Things to Know

Please leave your honest review of this book on Amazon and Goodreads. We appreciate your positive and constructive feedback. Thank you.

50 Things to Know

Printed in Great Britain
by Amazon